Mecca

By Martin Lings

THE ELEVENTH HOUR
The spiritual crisis of the modern world
in the light of tradition and prophecy

ANCIENT BELIEFS AND MODERN SUPERSTITIONS

COLLECTED POEMS
Revised and augmented

THE SECRET OF SHAKESPEARE
His greatest plays seen in the light of sacred art

THE QURANIC ART OF CALLIGRAPHY AND ILLUMINATION

THE BOOK OF CERTAINTY
The Sufi doctrine of faith, vision and gnosis

A SUFI SAINT OF THE TWENTIETH CENTURY
Shaykh Aḥmad al-ᶜAlawī: his spiritual heritage and legacy

WHAT IS SUFISM?

MUHAMMAD: HIS LIFE
BASED ON THE EARLIEST SOURCES

SYMBOL AND ARCHETYPE
A study of the meaning of existence

SPLENDOURS OF ISLAMIC CALLIGRAPHY
AND ILLUMINATION

Mecca

FROM BEFORE GENESIS
UNTIL NOW

Martin Lings

This first edition published in 2004 by
Archetype
Chetwynd House, Bartlow
Cambridge CB1 6PP, UK
www.archetype.uk.com

Distributed by Central Books Ltd., 99 Wallis Road, London EC9 5LN
www.centralbooks.com
In the US distributed by Midpoint Trade Books
www.midpointtradebooks.com

British Library Cataloguing in Publication Data
A catalogue record for this book is available from
The British Library

Typeset in Minion by Gilders Type
Printed and bound in Great Britain by St Edmundsbury Press,
Bury St Edmunds

FOR READERS IN A CHRISTIAN COUNTRY it is important to mention the immense difference between Revelation and inspiration, precisely because, for Christians as such, this question is not of first importance and for that very reason they may well have difficulty in understanding its vital importance for Jews and Muslims as also for older religions such as Hinduism. The word 'religion' means re-establishing the bond—the *lig*ament between man and God which man lost at the Fall. Every religion is thus something like a rope thrown down from Heaven for fallen man to cling to, and that rope is an aspect of the Divine Word which is mentioned in Christianity at the outset of St John's Gospel:

In the beginning was the Word, and the Word was with God, and the Word was God.

The Divine Word—as the rope which man must cling to—may take the form of a man or of a book.

1

Christ is by definition 'the Word made flesh', and being thus himself the actual lifeline which all Christians must cling to for their salvation, he is the very basis, the very root, of the Christian religion. But Moses is not the basis of Judaism, nor is Muḥammad the basis of Islam. They are the divinely chosen recipients of the Word made book, that is, in the case of Moses, the first five books of the Old Testament, the Pentateuch, and in the case of Muḥammad, the Qur'ān. Both these manifestations of the Divine Word are examples of Revelation as distinct from inspiration. Apart from the Pentateuch the Old Testament consists mainly of texts written under the inspiration of the Holy Spirit, and the same can be said of the whole of the New Testament. The presence of the Word made flesh leaves, in Christianity, no room for the Word made book, whereas in older, less simplified religions—Hinduism for example—there is room for both.

Revelation consists of the direct speech of God. That is why a revealed text has no ritual efficacy in a translation. It has to be spoken, if it forms part of a sacred rite, in the language in which it came down from Heaven. Let me say in passing that the definition of a sacred language is 'a language which God has spoken', in other words, a language which contains a Revelation. Examples which immediately come to mind are Sanskrit, Chinese, Hebrew and Arabic. Now as regards these last two languages and the Revelations which make them sacred, it is to be noticed in both that God's love seems to be given to no one more than to the Patriarch Abraham. The following passage is merely one of many which might be quoted from the Hebrew Revelation as evidence of this outstanding love:

> *I will bless thee and make thy name great; and thou shalt be a blessing ... and in thee shall all families of the earth be blessed* (Genesis, 12:2-3).

It is also highly significant that Christ, in referring to the immense felicity of the Afterlife, instead of simply saying 'in Paradise', should have used as synonym, on at least one occasion, the phrase 'in Abraham's bosom'. As to Islam, those of you who do not know Arabic have only to look up the name Abraham in the index of a Qur'ān translation and to follow up the multitude of references to him. Let it moreover be added that the Prophet Muḥammad, in speaking of the terrible state into which mankind would fall before the second coming of Christ, added by way of comfort the Divine promise that 'The earth shall not be found lacking in forty men whose hearts are as the heart of the Friend of God (*Khalīl Allāh*)', that is, Abraham. The word *Khalīl* is very strong and might more exactly be translated 'intimate friend'. Abraham is often spoken of in Islam simply as *al-Khalīl*; and that is why Hebron, in Palestine, where Abraham is buried, is also known to the Arabs as *al-Khalīl* by extension.

By this time, and probably before, some puzzled readers may have turned back once more to the title page to make certain that they are in fact reading a monograph which is entitled 'Mecca'. But let them be reassured that what they have read so far is not just a meaningless digression. Mecca is, beyond any doubt, the city of Abraham.

Abraham was one hundred years old when Sarah, aged ninety, gave birth to Isaac; and it was not long after this that she insisted, to Abraham, that his elder son Ishmael, and Hagar, the boy's mother, should no longer live with them. Abraham was very sorrowful at this, for he dearly loved Ishmael. But the book of Genesis tells us that God told him to follow the wishes of Sarah, promising that He Himself would be with Ishmael, and Abraham was altogether reassured. We are then told that Hagar took the child with her into the wilderness of Paran, that is, to the South. But when I said that most of the Old Testament after the Pentateuch is not Revelation, I said most rather than all; and the Qur'ān tells us, in the words of God:

Some of the Prophets We have favoured above others, and unto David We gave the Psalms. (17:55)

So David was the recipient of a Revelation; and in Psalm 84, which begins with the words: *How amiable are Thy tabernacles, O Lord of hosts,* there is a reference to Hagar and her son:

4

Blessed is the man whose strength is in Thee, in whose heart are the ways of them who passing through the valley of Baca make it a well. (5-6)

By an easy shift over the centuries from one labial consonant to another, that is, from B to M, the valley of Baca, in Arabic *Bakkah*, came to be called the valley of *Makkah*, in English, Mecca. The virtue in question here is trust in God to an altogether amazing degree, and the plural 'them' attributes it to the child as well as to his mother to indicate that Ishmael also was a personification of this virtue which earned, in the moment of dire necessity, the gushing forth of a spring from the earth of the barren valley. Genesis does not mention the valley or its name, but it tells us that *God heard the voice of the lad*, that is, Ishmael crying out for water as he lay in the sand, and of Hagar it says: *And God opened her eyes and she saw a well of water.* (21:17-20)

We are not told, and presumably we shall never know, how they reached that valley, some forty camel-days south of Canaan. But we may assume that they had no more choice about their subsequent movements than they had had about leaving Abraham's house. All we know is that the valley lay on one of the great caravan routes, the so-called 'incense route'. Travellers regularly passed through it on their way from the Mediterranean to South Arabia, and it could be that Hagar was guided to join one of the caravans and to leave it when the valley

5

had been reached. In the opposite direction, she could have sent Abraham a message. But in any case, message or no message, we may be sure that Abraham would not have been left in ignorance of where they were, for his presence in Baca was, as we shall see, a spiritual necessity.

The well and the spring that fed it came to be known as Zamzam. Its quenching of Ishmael's thirst was the first of innumerable blessings which have been destined to flow from it; and the miracle that made it gush forth may be said to mark the outset of God's establishment of a great place of pilgrimage. If a language is sacred because God has spoken it, a city is sacred because He has chosen and blessed the site of it. What is remarkable in this particular case is, as we have seen, the total absence of any human initiative.

Abraham had at that time still seventy years to live, and we may suppose that his visits to his son in the valley of Baca were not infrequent, for it was his God-given function to build there a sanctuary, to make it a place of pilgrimage, to act, with Ishmael, as host to the pilgrims, and to establish a line of spirituality in those parts as well as in Palestine. The Qur'ān tells us: *Verily the first sanctuary established for men is the house at Baca, a blessed place and a guidance for all the world.* (3:96)

The Qur'ān also tells us that God had shown Abraham the exact site, very near to the well of Zamzam, upon which he and Ishmael were to build the sanctuary. Its name, *Ka'bah* (cube), reflects its

shape which is a somewhat elongated cube, with its four corners facing East, North, West and South, this being the order in which they are visited in the seven anticlockwise rounds which constitute the pilgrimal rite of visitation. The North-East and South-West walls are slightly longer than the other two: and when the building was almost finished, an Angel brought to Abraham a stone which had fallen from Paradise on to the nearby hill Abu Qubays. According to the Prophet Muḥammad 'it descended from Paradise whiter than milk, but the sins of the sons of Adam made it black'. This celestial stone was built into the Eastern corner of the Kaʿba by Abraham and Ishmael, and it has always been considered as the most holy object in that holy place. The sanctuary was now ready for visitation, and Abraham was told: *Proclaim unto men the Pilgrimage, that they may come unto thee on foot and on every lean camel out of every deep ravine.* (Qur'ān 22:27)

Let us now consider some dates: the birth of Moses in 1699 BC seems to be generally accepted;

but of the two sets of dates—differing by a little more than one hundred and fifty years—which are assigned to the Patriarchs, the earlier ones seem to be definitely more acceptable than the later ones by which Joseph would still have had, at the birth of Moses in Egypt, sixty-four more years to live, whereas by the earlier dates his death preceded the birth of Moses by ninety-three years which are historically needed to allow certain developments to take place. According to these earlier dates Abraham was born in 2153 BC followed by Isaac one hundred years later. It would thus seem that the building of *the first sanctuary*, followed soon afterwards by the proclamation of the Pilgrimage to Baca, must have taken place approximately between 2030 BC and the turn of the millennium. The Ka‘ba is therefore about one thousand years older than the Temple of Jerusalem which was completed in 1007 BC in the reign of Solomon, who had succeeded his father David some ten years previously.

The Pilgrimage, proclaimed and established by Abraham and Ishmael about four thousand years ago, has continued to be performed until the present day. But the religion of Abraham as a whole was by its very nature exclusive, and it presupposed too much initial spirituality in its adherents to be able to grip a large community. There were always a few men and women who maintained the full purity of Abrahamic worship, and these were known as *Ḥunafā'*, plural of *ḥanīf*, 'orthodox', a title given to

Abraham in the Qur'ān. But this minority came to have less and less power in the land; and gradually over the centuries error began to prevail over truth in many domains. Not the least of the dangers lay in the idols which were sometimes brought by pilgrims from neighbouring tribes and offered as gifts, with assurances as to their great protective or otherwise beneficial powers, in return for the hospitality they themselves had received from the people of Baca; and it was when some of these idols were placed in the large open courtyard surrounding the Kaʿba that the Jews decided it was no longer spiritually profitable to visit this outlying tabernacle of Abraham. The reference to *Baca* in the Psalms is, however, an indication that its sanctuary must have been an object of great veneration for well over a millennium before the Jews felt obliged, for obvious reasons, to frequent it no longer. That decision did not concern other pilgrims; but the gradually dwindling minority of the *Ḥunafāʾ* could do nothing to protect their sanctuary; and the day came when a large idol named Hubal was placed inside the Kaʿba itself.

Idol worship was not, however, the only falling away from the religion of Abraham nor was it the worst. There is a danger which lurks in this lower world and which is always ready to come to the surface whenever religion is not faithfully and fully practised. Appearances are deceptive. Needless to say, we are not denying here the truth so eloquently

9

pointed out by Frithjof Schuon that 'the ideas of the Great Spirit and the primacy of the Invisible are natural to man'.[1] But when man himself degenerates further and further from his true nature, and when his inward consciousness of the Invisible becomes impoverished beyond a certain point, then the balance is likely to swing in favour of the primacy of the visible, of what the eye can see and the hand can touch. That becomes reality; and all else becomes questionable, and even improbable. By the end of the first millennium BC, despite the religion established by Moses, there had already come to be a sect among the Jews, Sadducees by name, who refused to believe in the Afterlife and in the existence of Angels. But this sect was too much of a minority to endanger Judaism as a whole, whereas in the land of the Ka'ba and the outlying Arab tribes that surrounded it on all sides, the esoterism of Abraham and Ishmael had not been supplemented by a religion which could meet the needs of the majority of the people; and there had come to be a widespread disbelief in the possibility of any life for man after the death of his body in this world.

There was, however, the clearest of signs, for anyone who had eyes to see, that all was not well: Zamzam had been lost. A tribe from the Yemen had briefly taken possession of Mecca, as it was beginning to be called, and when they were forced to leave they

[1] *From the Divine to the Human*, Bloomington, IN, 1981, p.6.

buried Zamzam, by way of revenge, before they left. Nor, even worse, did it occur to the Meccans themselves to undo this sacrilege and to recuperate the precious legacy left them by Ishmael. Many other wells had been dug, and they had enough water for their needs. After two generations had passed, the exact site of the holy well had been forgotten.

But God had promised Abraham and Hagar on more than one occasion that He would make Ishmael 'a great nation'. The lamentable situation we have just described was therefore doomed, sooner or later, to change; and in about AD 400 Quraysh, a powerful Arab tribe of Abrahamic descent, under the leadership of a man named Qusay, established themselves as rulers of Mecca. Qusay built himself a dwelling not far from the low wall which surrounded the courtyard of the Kaʿba and encouraged his sons and others of his tribe to follow his example. They were thus better able to look after the needs of the pilgrims, and they took very seriously their responsibility for this and for other duties related to their prestige as custodians of the Sanctuary. Nor did their ability in this respect fail to gain recognition from the other Arab tribes.

To say that they were highly principled would be a misuse of words. But if they could have read this statement they would, with one voice, have protested in amazement, pointing out that in their relations with each other and in the upbringing of their children they laid great emphasis on the principles of generosity, gratitude, courage, steadfastness, truth-telling, promise-keeping and other forms of reliability, not to speak of social considerations such as good manners and dignity of deportment. They could have been told, however, that their principles were lacking in height, confined to the horizontal plane, without any consciousness of the relationship between human virtues and the Divine Qualities of which they are the reflections. None the less, human virtues cannot exist without their archetypes, which is another way of saying that in these men the apparently missing link was not absent but dormant; and inevitably the degree of dormancy varied from man to man.

Within their tribes the Arabs would rejoice especially in the giftedness of outstanding members of their own particular clan. But the tribe as a whole needed its leaders, so that there was always a general recognition of a potential leader, whatever his clan. In Quraysh, among the grandsons of Qusay, there was one such man, Hāshim by name, who was held in considerable esteem not only by his own tribe but also by other Arab tribes. It was he who established, on the old incense route, the two great caravan journeys from Mecca, the Winter Caravan to the Yemen and the Summer Caravan to North-West Arabia and beyond it to Palestine and Syria; that is, to the outskirts of the Roman Empire. One of the first main halts of the Summer Caravan was the oasis of Yathrib, eleven camel-days north of Mecca; and

Hāshim made a proposal of marriage to a woman of one of the leading families of Yathrib. She accepted him on certain conditions, one of them being that if she bore him children she should keep them with her in the oasis. Hāshim agreed, and she bore him a son who, from an early age, showed himself to be remarkably gifted. Excellent reports of him were continually brought to Mecca, not only by his father who often went to see him, but by others whose judgement could be considered as altogether objective. Finally, after Hāshim's somewhat premature death when Shaybah—that was the boy's name— was only fourteen, Muṭṭalib, Hāshim's younger brother, decided to go to Yathrib and see his nephew face to face. Having taken upon himself Hāshim's heavy responsibility of acting as host to the pilgrims, he felt bound to foresee the day when he in his turn would need to lay the burden upon a successor. But none of his brother's three Meccan sons or his own sons showed much promise in that respect, nor had any of them a presence comparable to that of the young Yathribi Hāshimite whom he now set eyes upon for the first time. He was impelled then and there to ask Hāshim's widow to let him take Shaybah with him to his father's home. At first she refused, but Muṭṭalib was not to be gainsaid, and when he pointed out to her that much greater prospects awaited her son in Mecca than anything he could hope for in Yathrib, on condition that he first made himself something of a Meccan, for which there was now ample time, she saw that he had his nephew's welfare truly at heart and gave her consent. So some days later Muṭṭalib took Shaybah with him on the back of his camel; and when they rode into Mecca, one of the bystanders was heard to say to another: 'That must be a new slave that Muṭṭalib has bought'. Muṭṭalib indignantly corrected the speaker, but the story of the blunder went from mouth to mouth and caused so much merriment throughout the city that the name Shaybah was set on one side, and the new-comer came to be affectionately known as ʿAbd al-Muṭṭalib, the slave of Muṭṭalib, for the rest of his long and successful life.

All that his uncle had hoped for on his behalf was realised; and although, for Quraysh, there was no official chief of the tribe as there were chiefs of its different clans, ʿAbd al-Muṭṭalib in his late middle age was not only chief of the clan of Hāshim but was also generally looked up to as leader of the tribe as a whole; and when an army from the Yemen marched

against Mecca with the intention of destroying the Kaʿba, it was he who led a small group of Meccans to the Sanctuary, and it was he who took hold of the metal ring in the middle of the Kaʿba door and said: 'O God, Thy slave protecteth his house. Protect Thou Thy House!' His prayer was wonderfully answered.

But I am moving ahead too quickly. Many years before that episode ʿAbd al-Muṭṭalib came to be endowed—and we may venture to say providentially endowed—with a remarkable love for the Kaʿba itself. This grace may well have begun to develop soon after his arrival in Mecca. His function as assistant to his uncle, then as his successor, was all the more congenial to him on account of the frequent visits to the Sanctuary which it imposed upon him. But these visits were not enough, and in the prime of his life, when he already had one almost grown-up son and several daughters he would sometimes order a couch to be spread for him in the small precinct which adjoins the North-West wall of the Kaʿba and which itself is surrounded by a low semicircular wall. Beneath the stones which pave it lie the tombs of Ishmael and Hagar, and it is known as *Ḥijr Ismāʿīl*, the Sanctuary of Ishmael. Nor can one imagine a place better suited to the imperative command which he received in a vision when sleeping there. To be more precise, it was a series of visions, for he did not understand at first exactly what he had to do, and this obliged him to continue to sleep there on successive nights until everything was clarified. I have given a detailed account of this incident in my life of the Prophet,[1] and there is no need to repeat that here; nor is there need to dwell on other details of the life of ʿAbd al-Muṭṭalib which are also recorded in the same book. A brief outline must suffice us.

The command, accompanied by all the necessary information as to the exact place where the digging should begin was that he should restore the holy well of Zamzam. Not without difficulty he accomplished this task to perfection, with the help of his only son. But how much easier it would have been if he had had more sons! He prayed to God to give him ten more, promising that when they had all grown to manhood he would sacrifice one of them to Him at the Kaʿba.

The sons came, they all grew to manhood, and lots were drawn, by means of arrows, as to which of them should be sacrificed. The arrow which came out was that of ʿAbd Allāh, the youngest of the ten, his father's favourite, a youth of amazing beauty. ʿAbd al-Muṭṭalib drew out his knife, took ʿAbd Allāh by the hand and led him out of the Kaʿba towards the place of sacrifice in the courtyard. But meantime Fāṭimah, the young man's mother, had not been idle: three of the ten were her sons, so that she had already

[1] *Muhammad: His Life Based on the Earliest Sources*, Cambridge, 1986, chapters 4 and 5.

felt faced by the strong possibility that the victim might well be her own offspring. So when ʿAbd al-Muṭṭalib emerged from the Kaʿba he found himself faced by a large body of men of the powerful clan of Makhzūm, Fāṭimah's clan, determined to prevent the sacrifice of 'our sister's son'. ʿAbd al-Muṭṭalib began to tell them about his vow, but the chief of Makhzūm cut him short: 'Sacrifice him thou shalt not, but offer a sacrifice in his stead'; and he added that however costly the ransom might be, the clan of Makhzūm would pay for it. By this time ʿAbd Allāh's brothers had come out into the courtyard, and they added their pleas to those of the men of Makhzūm. ʿAbd al-Muṭṭalib longed to be persuaded, but he had powerful scruples. In the end however, after much prayer to God asking for clear signs of Divine acceptance, he was convinced that his son could be redeemed by a very costly sacrifice of camels. This was duly performed, and great was the rejoicing throughout Mecca that ʿAbd al-Muṭṭalib's son's life had been spared.

ʿAbd al-Muṭṭalib prayed to God, not to idols, but he tolerated the existence of idols, partly for reasons bound up with his function, which was concerned with the maintenance of a harmonious setting for the Pilgrimage and which made him averse to any changes which might disrupt that harmony. He was none the less nearer to the Ḥunafāʾ than any other of the leading men of Quraysh, and he had considerable respect for a cousin of his, Waraqah by name, who was generally considered to be one of the most eminent representatives of the tradition of Abraham.

Waraqah had in fact become a Christian, but that made no difference to his status as a Ḥanīf. It gave him the knowledge, however, that many of the Christians of those parts were expecting a prophet whose coming was held to be imminent. There were clear signs by which he would be recognisable, and these signs were mentioned in certain books which were well known to many prelates and other learned Christians of the Near East. I have never been able to find out the titles of any of them, let alone whether any of these manuscripts have survived. It was generally known, however, that one of the signs was that he would be a posthumous son, born to his mother after the death of his father; and since he would be the last prophet to be sent before the second coming of Christ, the seal of prophethood would be inscribed on his back in the form of a small but very distinctive mark between his shoulders.

It might seem surprising at first that there does not appear to have been any expectation of a prophet at that time in other parts of Christendom, but it was not in fact against the nature of things, or more precisely it was in the Divine economy of things, that his coming should not have been expected in places where he had no function to perform but only in that part of the world where he was destined to make himself felt and to establish his message.

It is, however, inconceivable, as Frithjof Schuon has said,[1] that in speaking of the future, Christ should have passed over in silence 'the one unique and incomparable apparition' which was to take place between his two comings; and there can be no doubt, if the following passage from the Gospel of St John be considered objectively, that it refers to the Prophet who is the theme of these last paragraphs, and who was, in fact, shortly to be born. The words of Christ are as follows:

> *I have more to tell you, but ye cannot bear it now. But when he, the spirit of truth, is come, he will tell you all things. He shall not speak of himself, but what he shall hear that shall he speak and he will show you things to come. He shall glorify me.*[2]

Like the Christians, the Jews of those parts were also certain that the advent of a prophet was very near, and they rejoiced in the expectation of his coming which would restore the balance of things and give them the upper hand over the Arabs, for he would of course be a Jew. How could it indeed be otherwise, since they were the 'chosen people'?

But Waraqah was far from such thoughts, for he saw that the Jews, whatever their faults might be, at least continued to believe in the Afterlife, nor did

[1] *The Transcendent Unity of Religions*, London, 1993, p.116.
[2] 16: 12-14.

they have idols, whereas the Arabs were desperately in need of a prophet. On the one hand there was the increasing belief amongst them of the finality of death, that death was the end of all things for the one who died. On the other hand, in a wide circle round the Kaʿba, there were three hundred and sixty idols, and almost every home in Mecca had its god, an idol large or small, the centre of the household: a man's last act on leaving home would be to go to the idol and stroke it to obtain blessings from it, and his first act on returning home would be the same. In less than six hundred years Christianity had transformed the Mediterranean and vast tracts of Europe. But it had made no real impact on the pagan society which centred on the Meccan sanctuary. Not that they were hostile to Christianity. A Christian had presented an icon of the Virgin and Child to the Kaʿba, and they had welcomed it as an addition of two more gods to those they already had. Nothing short of another Divine intervention would be capable of restoring spiritual law and order.

The life of ʿAbd al-Muṭṭalib's favourite son ʿAbd Allāh, which had been redeemed by the sacrifice of camels, was not destined to be spared for long. ʿAbd al-Muṭṭalib chose for him a bride from a clan of Quraysh near to his own, and soon after the marriage Āminah—that was her name—realised that she was expecting a child. The months passed, and the Summer caravan was soon due to pass through Mecca on its way to Syria and beyond. ʿAbd Allāh, who had reasons for going to those parts, decided to take advantage of the caravan, and on the way back when it stopped at the oasis of Yathrib, he lodged with the family of his grandmother. There he fell ill, the caravan had to go on without him, and after a few days he died.

Āminah's great consolation was the babe in her womb, and one night she was told in a vision that it was a boy, and that he should be named *Muḥammad*. She herself died some four years later, and ʿAbd al-Muṭṭalib took charge of his orphaned grandson until he himself died when the boy was only seven. He was brought up by his father's full brother Abū Ṭālib, and at the age of twenty-five he married a near relation of Waraqah, a widow some fifteen years older than himself, a woman of great beauty and wisdom, Khadījah by name. Their marriage was exceedingly happy.

It was when he was about forty years old, during a spiritual retreat in a cave on the outskirts of Mecca, that he received the first Revelation of verses from the Qur'ān, which were uttered to him by the Archangel Gabriel, who also gave him to understand that he, Muḥammad, was the Messenger of God. Throughout the rest of his life he continued to receive revelations until the Qur'ān was complete, but it soon became clear that he had the mandate from Heaven to establish a new religion on the basis of what was gradually revealed to him. This new religion, Islam by name, strongly confirmed both

Judaism and Christianity, while being itself, as the revelations maintained, more Abrahamic than either of these two religions which had preceded it.

Before the beginning of his prophethood, Muḥammad had been looked on unanimously by the leaders of Quraysh as the most promising man of his own generation, a man eminently capable of increasing the prestige of Quraysh among the other Arab tribes, and, beyond that, of enhancing the respect felt by other nations for the Arabs as a whole. He had come to be generally known throughout Mecca as '*al-Amīn*', a word often translated as 'the Honest', though this falls short of the total trustworthiness and reliability which it conveys. But when he began to make known his mandate, the chiefs of the clans of Quraysh to a man were averse to his message. Needless to say, it is not in the nature of things that Heaven should allow a Prophet, authorised to establish a new religion, to be born into this world without enriching at the same time his generation with a number of other highly gifted men and women qualified to support him. But apart from this small minority, his first adherents, as far as concerned the great families, were mostly younger sons who had no political prospects, and there were also a number of slaves. These converts were far outnumbered by an implacably hostile and at the same time powerful majority. Among the pilgrims, however, who came to Mecca there were also converts; these included an increasing group of men from Yathrib; and finally, when the opposition in

Mecca became so strong that the Prophet's life was in danger, the Archangel told him to accept a pressing invitation to go and live in the oasis where his grandfather had been born and bred.

In Mecca the Muslims, that is, the adherents of Islam, had been ordered to be facing towards Jerusalem when they prayed the ritual prayer. But not long after the Prophet's emigration to Yathrib this orientation was changed, and the Qur'ān ordered them to face in the opposite direction, towards Mecca. As to the leaders of Quraysh, whatever conclusions they may have drawn from this change, they were above all dismayed by the safe establishment of Muḥammad in Yathrib, beyond their immediate reach, which made them more than ever conscious that their way of life was endangered by the new religion, and more than ever bent on destroying it before it was too late. To this end, on three successive occasions, armies considerably outnumbering any force that the Muslims could muster had set out from Mecca, but each time they were frustrated by the unseen Angels who were fighting against them.

Meantime the Revelation had added an entirely Abrahamic dimension to Islam, namely the Pilgrimage to Mecca. There had always been two pilgrimal rites, the Pigrimage proper, *al-Ḥajj*, which could only be made on the tenth day of the twelfth and last month of the lunar year, and the lesser Pilgrimage known as the Visitation, *al-ʿUmrah*, which could be made at any hour of any day throughout the year. Not long after the third and last onslaught of Quraysh against the Muslims, the Prophet had a vision which prompted him to make the lesser Pilgrimage.

He set out for Mecca with a large body of his followers, and news of their approach was immediately sent on horseback to the Meccans by their confederates in the neighbouring tribes. It was as if Abraham had intervened to make peace between his descendants; and for the moment, looked at objectively, the situation was not without its humour: the leaders of Quraysh found themselves suddenly in what was, for them, an appalling and totally unexpected dilemma. As guardians of the Kaʿba it was their function to welcome all the pilgrims who came to Mecca. No would-be pilgrim had ever been refused admission to the Sanctuary. The problem seemed altogether insoluble, and to gain time they sent a chief of one of their clans together with two of his clansmen to meet the Muslims at the very edge of the sacred precinct, before they entered it, and to make a treaty with them that if they would return home immediately without proceeding any further, they should be allowed, in one year's time, to make the lesser Pilgrimage unimpeded.

The treaty also put an end to all the fighting between them for ten years provided that certain conditions laid down were not broken, and it specified that outlying tribes, confederates of Quraysh or confederates of the Muslims, could also join in this pact. The Prophet agreed to everything, and the treaty was also signed by representatives of two other tribes, one on each side.

The Muslims performed the lesser Pilgrimage the following year, and as Quraysh had feared this was seen far and wide as a great triumph for the new religion. It also served to demonstrate its Abrahamic nature; and there were many converts from different parts of Arabia, including even some influential Meccans themselves who had previously fought against Islam.

Then suddenly, to add to the dismay of Quraysh, the treaty was broken and thereby nullified: their confederate tribe attacked the tribe confederate with Yathrib, whereupon the victims of the attack immediately appealed to the Prophet to right the wrong, and he set out for the South with a far larger army than anything that Quraysh could now muster. Without any actual declaration of war, and having sent word ahead that those who took refuge in the Sanctuary or in their own homes would be safe, he entered Mecca with the main body of his army. Its right wing, momentarily separated from the rest, encountered and put to flight what little resistance there was with the loss of only two men, as compared with thirty of Quraysh.

The Prophet went straight to the Sanctuary, where he addressed the multitude of those taking refuge there. He spoke to them the words, quoted from the Qur'ān, which Joseph had spoken to his brothers in Egypt when they finally realised who he was: Verily I say as my brother Joseph said: *This day there shall be no upbraiding of you nor reproach. God forgiveth you, and He is the Mercifullest of the merciful* (12:92). He then gave orders that Hubal and the idols round the Ka'ba, as well as all the household idols should be destroyed.

Meantime more and more of those who had taken refuge in their homes were coming to the Sanctuary, and the Prophet withdrew to the lower slopes of the hill of Ṣafā just outside the wall surrounding the courtyard of the Ka'ba. There he received the homage of those of his enemies who now wished to enter Islam, both men and women, and they came to him in hundreds.

When he had set out from Medina, he had not let it be known, even to his troops, that Mecca was his objective, while at the same time he had encouraged various false rumours, one of these being that he was out to attack the powerful Hawāzin tribe and their confederates, all of whom were devotees of the so-called goddess al-Lāt whose shrine at Ṭā'if, only a short distance south of Mecca, had long been one of the three most spellbinding centres of idolatry in Arabia. As soon as they heard that Muḥammad had marched out against them they had begun to consolidate their army, nor had they ceased to do so when it became clear that his immediate goal was Mecca, for in addition to his destruction of the idols there he had sent to destroy the temple of al-ʿUzzah, the nearest to Mecca of the three 'great' shrines, having already destroyed the one nearest to Medina, that of Manāt. Their beloved 'Lady of Ṭā'if' alone remained and they were determined to defend her.

After two weeks in Mecca the Prophet set out to meet them, and his army was now strengthened by every Meccan man of fighting age, for even those who had not yet entered Islam were out to defend their city against Hawāzin. The battle which ensued went first of all against the Muslims, but the Prophet and those of the Companions nearest him held their ground, and uttering a prayer he took some pebbles and threw them at the enemy as he had done at Badr. This time the Angels were unseen, but the rout of the enemy was tremendous, as were the spoils which included six thousand women and children who had been behind the lines with about twenty-four thousand camels and innumerable sheep and goats.

They set siege to Ṭā'if, but after some days the Prophet decided that this was not the way to overcome Thaqīf who were defending it and their goddess, so he raised the siege. But as the army was marching away, a plea of one of his men that he should put a curse on the city's defenders prompted him to the opposite and he raised his hands in prayer that God should give him the men of Thaqīf. In due course the prayer was answered: Thaqīf entered Islam and the shrine of al-Lāt, the third and last of the strongholds of Arab idolatry, was destroyed together with all the household idols of Ṭā'if. The details of this, by no means without interest, are recorded in my book,[1] but they have no direct relevance to our theme here.

Meantime the raising of the siege precluded any call for immediate fighting in the region of Mecca, and in this connection it is important to understand that the bulk of those who had come there with the Prophet, that is, the Muslims of Yathrib, consisted in the main of two groups: the refugees, mostly Meccans in origin, were known as the Emigrants, whereas the Yathribis themselves were known as the Helpers in view of their immense hospitality and all else that they had done in support of the new religion. The Helpers were now afraid that having gained possession of his own native city the Prophet would stay there and not return with them to their oasis. Nor, to say the least, would their fears have been lessened if they had known that the Prophet had said on looking back towards Mecca just after leaving it for Yathrib: 'Of all

_____

[1] *Muhammad*, chapter 80.

God's earth thou art the dearest place unto me and the dearest unto God, and had my people not driven me out from thee I would not have left thee.'

The fears of the Helpers were none the less increased by something that they knew very well, namely that the strangers to the oasis were particularly susceptible to its fever, whereas the Yathribis themselves were much less prone to it and in some cases even immune. Nor would they have forgotten that a few years previously there had been a severe epidemic of the fever to which many of the Emigrants had succumbed. There were no deaths but a wave of homesickness for Mecca had swept over their refugee guests. They did not however know that in consequence of this the Prophet had felt impelled to pray: 'O God, make Medina as dear unto us as Thou hast made Mecca, or even dearer. And bless for us its waters and its grain, and carry away from it its fever.' And God answered his prayer. So when the time came for the return of the army to Medina, it was the Prophet who led them back, with assurances that he would never forsake them, and none of the Emigrants remained behind. Not that the nostalgia for Mecca had been extinguished, but it had been raised to a sacramental level and thereby de-individualized.

The establishment of the new Islamic orientation in the direction of Mecca needed, to be altogether effective, a consciousness on the part of these first Muslims that their actual home was at a certain distance from Mecca. To become fully incorporated into Islam, the Abrahamic dimension of the Pilgrimage needed to be performed by the Prophet of the new religion, in order that his performance of it could be recorded in full detail for future genera- tions. It is true that ever since the time of Abraham the Pilgrimage has been performed by inhabitants of Mecca. But from the point of view of a world religion such performances are the exception rather than the norm, and what was needed was a normal pilgrim- age. This was duly performed by Muḥammad in the last year of his life.

It was at the same time necessary that the Seal of the Prophets should have a city which belonged to him in particular; and this had in fact been virtually the case from the moment when the Archangel had told him to accept the Yathribi invitation to go and live in the oasis. Let us briefly retrace the events: after a perilous journey, protected by miracles, he finally arrived in Quba at the southern edge of the oasis together with his companion Abū Bakr and their Bedouin guide, a man who was familiar with out-of- the-way tracks such as only a true son of the desert would know. Each of the normally used northward routes from Mecca was being patrolled on horseback by organised groups of Quraysh determined to pre- vent the safe establishment of their common enemy beyond their reach.

After a few days in Quba, knowing that they were eagerly awaited in the most closely inhabited part of the oasis, the Prophet gave the word to set out once more, this time to their final destination. He himself was mounted on his camel Qaṣwā', and it was she who set the slow and stately pace of the procession, which consisted not only of the newcomers but also all those who had come to meet them halfway; and they were welcomed by cries of rejoicing 'Come is the Prophet of God' which increased as more and more men, women and children lined the way of approach. More than once it happened that a man or group of clansmen took hold of Qaṣwā's halter and begged the Prophet to alight there and be their guest, but each time, having given them his blessing, he said: 'let her go her way, for she is under the command of God.' Finally she turned from the road and went into a large walled courtyard. There at the entrance to an enclosure that was used for prayer she knelt, and the Prophet let go her rein but did not alight. Then she rose to her feet and began to walk slowly away; but she had not gone far when she stopped, turned in her tracks and walked back to where she had first knelt. Then she knelt again, but this time she flattened her chest against the ground, whereupon the Prophet alighted and said: 'This if God will, is the dwelling.'

We are reminded here of the absence of human initiative which had characterised the Divine choice of the centre upon which the Kaʿba was to be built. Its local designation, 'the city', in Arabic *al-Madīnah*, was destined to become the worldwide name of the cluster of dwellings, some of which were already there, others yet to be built around the centre which Qaṣwā' had chosen, under Divine inspiration, for the abode of the Prophet, that is, his house and his mosque. As to his house, the room in which he died is now his tomb, and what lies between that and the pulpit of the Mosque is held to be a particularly blessed part of that hallowed site owing to his words: 'The space between my grave and my pulpit is a garden (*rawḍah*) among the gardens of Paradise.'

A visit to Medina is made by the majority of pilgrims to Mecca, but it is in no sense a part of the pilgrimal rite, nor do the visitants need any preparatory instructions. As in other religions, every territory in the Islamic world has its patron saint, and in addition to his or her tomb there are many other tombs of saints which have been regularly visited by Muslims throughout the centuries. Of all these the tomb in Medina is beyond question the holiest, but like others it demands no more from the visitant than what is a matter of spiritual common sense. More precisely, it demands that the soul shall muster up all the piety it is capable of, or in other words that it shall be, as far as it can, a personification of humility, sense of the sacred, charity and otherworldliness. To make this effort may be said to open the way for the soul to develop, as it were, an extra dimension. Needless to say, the Pilgrimage likewise makes these demands; and as to the extra dimension, its development is, as we shall see, immeasurably facilitated by being imposed on the pilgrim in a literal sense.

This new dimension begins to make itself keenly felt with the donning of the pilgrim's dress when a certain proximity to the sacred precinct has been reached, from whatever direction that may be. The state of what is called *iḥrām*, which could be translated 'consecration' or 'dedicated abstinence', has to be formally entered. Its conditions include, apart from wearing special garments, keeping a watch over one's tongue. Not silence but a certain taciturnity is imposed: there must be no idle chattering, no entering into anything like a heated argument, and no manifestations of anger. Other conditions—and I will not mention them all—include not hunting any wild animals for food, and not killing any wild animals or insects except such as might be dangerous.

Originally there was, for both sexes, an alternative to clothes, namely a return to the nakedness of primordial man. This remained a fully approved mode of *iḥrām* until, in the last few years of the Prophet's life, the Pilgrimage not only became an Islamic rite but it also became one of the five pillars of Islam, and according to what the Revelation had already laid down with regard to dress, a woman's body had to be entirely covered, including the head, in the presence of any men who were not of her nearest of kin. The Abrahamic tradition continued however to prevail in the ruling that the faces and hands of women must not be covered during the Pilgrimage.

As to male dress, there was nothing in the Qur'anic law which raised any problems, and to this day men continue to wear the full traditional pre-Islamic pilgrim's dress; but as to the traditional alternative, like certain other already mentioned aspects of the precious legacy of the first of the Patriarchs, sacred nudity presupposes a spiritual development which could not be said to characterise more than a very small minority in any one of those three religions which are, in a sense, Abraham's legatees. There could therefore have been no question of Islam's retaining nakedness as the pilgrimal alternative to clothing.

The clothes, so it is said, should be light in colour, and in fact most pilgrims, especially the men, wear white. Men must be bare-headed, and they must also be bare-heeled which means wearing a special kind of sandal. Their dress consists of two pieces of cloth, neither of which may have a single stitch of sewing in it. One of these is girded round the waist and must be broad enough to hang well below the knees; the other, about a yard in breadth and at least three yards long, is draped over the left shoulder so that one end hangs down in front almost to the ground. The other end is passed round the back, under the right arm leaving that arm and shoulder bare, and then passed across the chest and thrown over the left shoulder so as to hang down the back. This is how it must be worn when the pilgrimal rites are being performed, but at other times most of the pilgrims cover the

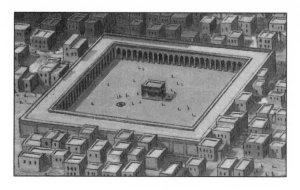

right shoulder and the arm with it as well as the left. Not a few of them buy this longer cloth with a twofold purpose, firstly to wear it on the pilgrimage, perhaps more than once, and finally to wear it as a shroud. In any case the pilgrims are exhorted to keep death continually in mind.

I myself have had the privilege of making the Pilgrimage twice, in 1948 and in 1976, and it will not be out of place to quote here a passage from a letter I wrote to a friend immediately after the first of these two Pilgrimages, that is, fifty-five years ago. I had already mentioned how my wife and I had reached Mecca after midnight and how in the small hours, we had made our first pilgrimal visit to the Kaᶜba and performed the rite of *tawāf* (circumambulation) which consists of seven anticlockwise circuits starting at the Eastern corner of the Kaᶜba, that is, the corner of the Black Stone, and then finally making a supplication in front of the door of the Kaᶜba which is a little to the right of the Stone. We had then withdrawn to the edge of the central precinct where, enshrined like a miniature tomb, there is a small rock which has in it the imprint of feet. The Qur'ān refers to it as *Maqām Ibrāhīm*, the station of Abraham. It was originally beside the Kaᶜba but it had to be moved to its present place so as not to impede the flow of the pilgrims making their rounds. While building the Kaᶜba Abraham had been standing on this rock, and his feet had imprinted themselves in it owing to the weight of a heavy stone handed him by Ishmael.

Having prayed in front of this Maqām we went to the Well of Zamzam, to which, at that time, there was access only a few paces from the Maqām. We were each given a vessel of the holy water, and when I had drunk I poured what was left over my head. We then had to perform, as an essential part of the Pilgrimage, the rite of following the footsteps of Hagar as she hastened seven times between Ṣafā and Marwah, two nearby rocky mounds, to see if anyone was in sight who could help her to find water.

I now begin the quotation from my letter:

By the time I had drunk from the water of Zamzam I was beginning to be more and more conscious of something which every pilgrim to Mecca is bound to feel in some degree or other. All Muslims are of course told of the Pilgrimage from their earliest years, and they see members of their family or of neighbouring families set off for Mecca and hear them

recount their experiences when they return. But this voluntary rite, which the majority of Muslims are never able to perform, remains none the less a secret dimension in Islam, hidden from all those who have not actually explored it for themselves; and this dimension is the link between the present moment and the past. It is by no means only in virtue of the Pilgrimage that Islam is named 'the primordial religion', but the Pilgrimage is an eloquent demonstration of what these names imply, for it is not only a journey in space to the centre towards which one has always turned one's face in prayers, but also a journey in time far back beyond the missions of Muḥammad, Jesus and Moses. Consciousness of this 'regress' in time was heightened for most of us by the feeling of a return to childhood: all except those few who have made a special study of the rites suddenly find themselves snatched from a relative mastery of their religion and placed again in a state of utter dependence on others, quite helpless in themselves and having to be told what to do and say at almost every turn. 'This is not the Islam that I know' is a thought that must occur to many. But that is only incidental whereas the return to the far past imposes itself upon everyone even, and perhaps above all, on those who are familiar with the rites.

Strangely archaic, in pre-Islamic Arabic, is the pilgrim's acknowledgement of their over-whelming sense of the Presence of God, which impels them to greet Him, *Labbaik Allahumma Labbaik* (Here I am, O God, at Thy service, here at Thy service) a greeting which is used at no other time and which can even replace that so characteristic feature of Islam, the greeting of Peace, and one is keenly aware that Mecca is the city of Abraham. Moreover, as we have already seen, unlike the other pillars of the religion, the Pilgrimage rites were not newly instituted at the outset of Islam. The Qur'ān confirms them, but they were instituted by Abraham; and for him they were a return to the past. The return to him is thus only the starting point of the Pilgrimage, a point from which, as we shall see, it sets out into a still remoter past.

We left the mosque by the gate of Ṣafā in order to visit Ṣafā itself, about two minutes' walk away. From Ṣafā we went to Marwah, a similar rocky eminence almost a quarter of a mile distant, and then back again to Ṣafā, going between the two seven times, mostly walking but always breaking into a run between the two points where our way—still, in those days, the sand track upon which the Prophet himself had walked—came nearest to the well of Zamzam. As we went back again to

Ṣafā we met, coming back to Marwah, those who had been coming from Marwah when we were on our way to it, and at each course we would meet many familiar figures moving in the opposite direction, always with the addition of newcomers. It was like a strange and marvellous dream as if those whom we encountered had stepped from the pages of Genesis, men and women whose lives were dominated by the testification to Islam in its Abrahamic form. *There is no god but God; Abraham is the messenger of God.* It was especially remarkable to see the Arabs themselves as they are to be seen at no other time, with nothing to hide their hair which most of them wear long. No doubt many if not most of these were from remote Arab villages into which the modern world had not penetrated. There were patriarchal old men with flowing white hair and beards, and men of middle age, and also no lack of young men, some of them scarcely more than boys. Among the Arabs one takes majesty of bearing for granted, but I was none the less struck by the wonderful dignity and grave solemnity of the young; and as they drew nearer one realised that they stood not only for the beauty of youth but also for the beauty of a proud and noble race and the beauty of a relatively uncontaminated theocratic civilisation.

That is all I will quote from my letter, having in fact already quoted too much, since all that I wished to convey was that when the Pilgrims reach Mecca they encounter Abraham, each according to his or her readiness and receptivity. Then having done so they accompany him to a still more remote past.

On the eighth day of the month, some on foot, others on camels, but most of them in cars, they set off for Mina, a small barren valley partly surrounded by rocky hills almost six miles to the East of Mecca but still within the Sacred Precinct. They spend the night there, in tents which they bring with them or in the open as the case may be, and the next morning they set out for Mount Arafat where they are obliged to be for part of the day and part of the night. We spent some hours there in a tent, and in the late afternoon, when the great heat had cooled a little, we walked to one of the higher parts of the Mount which is known as the Mount of Mercy. This is, in time, the most remote point of the Pilgrimage, for if Mecca is the city if Abraham, Arafat is sacred to Adam, and the

pilgrims go to the Mount of Mercy to be, despite the crowds, alone with God and to renew, each one for himself or herself, the forgiveness and mercy which God gave to Adam after the Fall.

In virtue of its Adamic associations Arafat is not included within the Sacred Precinct since its pilgrimal function is to remind us of primordial nature which cannot admit of any circumscription. In order to be there at night as well as in the day the Pilgrims remain on the Mount for about twenty minutes after sunset. Then they return to the Precinct and spend the night in the open, mostly in supplication, returning to their tents in Mina after the dawn prayer or before. I will say no more about the details of the Pilgrimage except that it ends—nor could it be otherwise—with seven concluding rounds of the Ka ͨba.

Since Arafat stands beyond Mecca in both time and space, why is the Pilgrimage not known as the Pilgrimage to Arafat? By way of answer it could be said that Arafat is a prolongation of Mecca, an aspect of it, but not its holiest aspect which is, as we have seen, the Black Stone. A more general answer is that religion depends for its existence on two elements, one of which is vertical and the other horizontal, Revelation to establish it, and Tradition to maintain it throughout the centuries. The existence of Mecca as a spiritual centre is inseparable from the vertical element, the Divine Revelation of religion to Abraham and Ishmael. But the association of Arafat with Adam has been handed down by Tradition; and, spiritually speaking, the vertical always takes precedence over the horizontal. In England when Muslims turn, at the time of prayer, towards Mecca, they happen to be turning also towards Arafat. But needless to say, when the pilgrims are between Mecca and Arafat, they face towards the Ka'ba, with their backs to the mountain.

There can be no doubt that the essence of discernment lies in discerning the difference between the Absolute and the relative. This is continually affirmed throughout the writings of Frithjof Schuon, who also affirms that this discernment includes, in a secondary way, as regards the domain of relativity, an awareness of the imprints of the Absolute upon the relative. For us the domain of relativity in question can be nothing other than this lower world, the world of the body and the soul in which we live, since we have no access to any higher levels of relativity except by special inspiration.

The importance of this awareness is stressed in the Qur'ān, which makes it clear that there can be no piety without reverent recognition of 'the signs of God' in the world about us. Some of these signs— these imprints of the Absolute—are to be seen in the marvels of virgin nature; others are to be seen in the religions, in the Divine Messengers who have been sent to establish them, and in the Saints who have perpetuated them. We could go on giving example after example, but let us limit ourselves to the example that our context demands, namely the sacred cities of the world.

There are now no sacred cities in the continent of Europe, but there is one within relatively easy reach of its south-eastern borders. Not very far inland from the Asian coast which bounds the Mediterranean at its eastern end there stands what is, for the vast majority of Europeans (including those who have taken possession of the two Americas), the city of cities. Nor is the sacred city of this book very far to the south of that city; and between them there is, as we have seen, yet a third sacred city.

We are accustomed to speaking of the Holy Land, but our conception of it should be extended, objectivly speaking, as far as Mecca, just as the Land itself was extended by the Heaven-directed journey of Hagar and Ishmael with a view to the establishment of the oldest of the three sanctuaries.

This hallowing of that narrow strip of earth at the extreme Western edge of Asia was soon to be followed by another hallowing, by the to-and-fro journeys of Abraham between his sons, between the land of Canaan and the valley of Baca; and these blessed signs were finally consummated by the miraculous night-journey of Muḥammad on the Heaven-sent steed Burāq, accompanied by the Archangel Gabriel on foot, from the Kaʿba to the site of Solomon's Temple, where he was met by all the Biblical prophets and whence, from a rock on the site of the Temple, he was taken up by Burāq,

44

still accompanied by the Archangel, to the highest Heaven, and back again to the Kaʿba in time to pray there the dawn prayer, a miracle referred to in the Qur'ān, in the opening verse of a chapter which, in consequence, is often named 'The Night Journey':

Glory be to Him who took His slave by night from the inviolable Mosque unto that furthest Mosque whose precincts We have made blessed. (17:9)

The word 'mosque' is an anglicised form of the Arabic *masjid* (literally 'place of prostration'). In the Qur'ān it has no exclusively Islamic significance, and 'the furthest Mosque' is the whole site of the Temple. The mosque on that site which is now known as 'the furthest Mosque' had yet to be built.

In conclusion let it simply be added, with regard to the religions which are as it were rooted in Abraham, that the city of Jerusalem is of immense importance to all three of them, to each in its own particular way. The city of Medina on the other hand belongs to Islam alone; but this cannot be said of Mecca, even sacramentally speaking, for the Psalms are among the greatest treasures of both Judaism and Christianity, and Baca is, as we have seen, extolled in the Psalms as one of the 'Lovable tabernacles' of God.

It is true that the vast majority of both Jews and Christians are unaware of the identity in question, but nevertheless, and despite centuries of hostility to Islam and therefore to its prophet, Mecca is universally recognised as a place of superlative importance, so much so that the name itself is suggestive of an excellence that cannot be surpassed.

Moreover the truth has its rights, and it will sometimes subtly and unobtrusively assert itself over error. There are many prophets and many pilgrimages; but just as the two words 'the Prophet' have come in common parlance to be a synonym for Muḥammad, so also 'the Pilgrimage' is taken as a matter of course to refer to that pilgrimage which has been performed, as far as we know without a break, for the last four thousand years.◈